Pull The Nail?

What is Stopping You

by

Lindsay Graham

Copyright © 2014

Second edition date 10/01/14

ISBN 1502514516

Cover Photograph Tom Graham

*"The experienced mountain climber is not
 intimidated by a mountain – he is inspired by it.
The persistent winner is not discouraged by a
problem – he is challenged by it.
Mountains are created to be conquered;
adversities are designed to be defeated;
problems are sent to be solved. It is
better to master one mountain than a thousand foothills."*
                    William Arthur Ward

To Glen Torrence
Born 5/11/27
Advanced 7/6/09

Hey, Glen Torrence I know you are watching from above! I wrote <u>Pull the Nail</u> for advancing life and mostly because of you. Glen, you planted the seed in my youth. You challenged me with your statement; "No one can make you mad but yourself."

I had a hard time believing that concept as a youth of 14 years. I now fully understand the principle, but to be honest, at times I still struggle with practicing it. Your statement was the seed that germinated into a lifelong love for each other. That seed is still bearing fruit and will continue to bear fruit.

Now, I must quit typing. There is something in my eyes. I can't see the keyboard and it is getting wet.

Thank you, Glen, for being my mentor and guide, and for always displaying your true self -- LOVE !

FORWARD

We received the phone call in the evening. The man on the other end of the line worked with our daughter at a small, private boarding school in North Carolina. He informed my wife that our daughter had just been in an accident and had been life-flighted to the trauma unit of a hospital not far from where the accident occurred. All we were told in that call was that she was alive, but unconscious. She was apparently in a coma. We knew nothing more than that.

Subsequent phone calls from us, in Ohio, to doctors and nurses in Tennessee, told us that Sarah was in critical condition - and that her death, at the age of 23, was very possible, if not imminent. If she escaped death, other possibilities sounded only slightly better for a young woman who loved running, biking, mountain climbing, and hard, physical work: At one point her doctor said that the likely outcome of an accident such as hers was total paralysis of the right side of her entire body.

This event was a game-changer for me, in more ways than one. First, this accident painted it clear in my mind how one simple decision can greatly impact not only your life, but the lives of everyone who loves you. Sarah's simple decision? She had decided to ride her bicycle without wearing a helmet. Each decision you make definitely leaves ripples in the pond of your life.

Also in more ways than one, this story has happy "endings." Sarah survived. That is happy enough. But she did not just survive; she thrived. She is not paralyzed - not at all. She has full function of her entire body and all her mental faculties are intact as well. Not only that, but she returned to work just three months after an accident that doctors said should have either killed her, paralyzed her, or sent her to therapy for no less than a year. My daughter is a walking miracle.

What really changed for me, though, was my emotional life. Sarah's accident was horrible. I experienced every level of fear, sadness, disappointment, discouragement and angst. As she conquered tests and barriers to recovery, I became elated and joyous, hopeful and grateful.

As she continued to improve, I found myself examining how I had spent a significant portion of my life suppressing emotions, denying my needs, and not really living. Through self- examination, I discovered several nails that had not been pulled; wounds I had let guide my decisions, my life, the stories I told others.

Lindsay Graham's book contains necessary messages about how we all, in one-way or another, have had a nail shot through our thumbs - or maybe through our hearts. It points out that it is never too late, however, to pull out those nails, even if it takes a 3-1/2 foot crow bar.

As I started the work of pulling my nails, I began to feel alive in ways I had never experienced. I found love and connection that I had never felt before. Pulling these nails is more like being reborn than it is like minor surgery. I sincerely request that you not wait for a near-death experience of yourself or a loved one.

Take a careful look for those long neglected spikes and splinters, or the mote in your eye. If you're alive, as Lindsay says, you probably have them.

The life you really want really is waiting for you. And it's more marvelous than you even imagine. Truly, what is stopping you?

Ken Matesz
September 2014

Ken Matesz is the author of two books, Masonry Heaters, Designing, Building and Living with a Piece of the Sun, published in 2010 by Chelsea Green Publishing Company, and Creating a Craftsman, scheduled for publication in late 2014. He is self-employed, designing and building masonry heaters, writing, living and loving life in northwest Ohio.

TABLE OF CONTENTS

PREFACE

Welcome to <u>Pull the Nail</u> (PTN). The journey to write this book has been a long and beautiful one. <u>PTN</u> comes from 40 years of searching for my core and seeking the universal truths of life that resonate with me. <u>PTN</u> is a collection of observations and principles revealed from my search. The lesson that appeared before me over and over again was that God always invites us to expand and grow. This invitation, this communication, can be received by anyone at anytime.

We have to be willing to listen, and be open to feel, the message. This communication is not reserved for just the one who meditates on the mountaintop or the people sitting in church pews. You see, most of the time the voice comes from within. The invitation is generally spoken in ordinary language, seldom is it communicated with a lightening bolt. I have learned that the most important principle of life is that we are not our past. <u>PTN</u> is written with this in mind, emphasizing the importance of first dropping the false story of our past. Far too many people live their restrictive story and not their unlimited life.

What does <u>PTN</u> offer you? <u>PTN</u> offers you, the reader, a new perspective on your life in a unique way. PTN will directly involve you and ask questions that maybe you have never thought of before. <u>PTN</u> invites you to reflect on the answers to these questions and their meanings. What meanings do we carry that are just not serving us anymore? We will look at the high cost to each of us of carrying and doing things that no longer serve us! Please stay with the journey and I will offer methods to effect positive change.

1

My journey in life led me full circle back to me. Deep inside, as I was walking the path, I knew this would happen. What do I mean by full circle back to me? My journey, as with anyone's journey, led me back to my own greatness, my own human potential. We all find everything we need inside of ourselves. We merely need to hush our inner critic and seek our core truth.

Acknowledgements
Thank you to my beautiful bride, Kathy, for becoming a book widow while I wrote. I see how my past has prevented me from cherishing her. Never again!
Thank you to Kim Lehman for his hours of formatting and pre-editing my work.
Thank you to Teri Bersee for capturing the message with her outstanding illustrations.
I would like to thank my pre-readers Carole, Jerry, Joy, Ken, Duke, and Teri.

Thank you Ken Matesz for the heartfelt Forward to this book. While writing this book, I received the news of your daughter's grave injury. I remember how elated you were when you told me, days after the accident that Sarah moved her thumb for you on command. I remember thinking, "Here I am writing this book about life's problems, and your experience sure puts priorities in perspective."

I would like to also thank Kim for his friendship and for telling me several times over the years that I could and would write a book. I didn't see that reality because I was stuck in my limiting belief. In hindsight, I see that God was inviting me to expand and grow through those gentle reminders that I was an author. You see, I kept rejecting those original invitations. To wake me up, God bypassed the middleman and made the invite a little stronger. His stronger message has a lot to do with the cover photograph and everything to do with Chapter One. So yes, I finally got the message! I hope you enjoy it.

INTRODUCTION

"Many of us are afraid to follow our passions,
to pursue what we want most because it
means taking risks and even facing failure.
But to pursue your passion with all your heart
and soul is success in itself. The greatest failure
is to have never really tried."

Robin Allen

Well, here you are wondering whether you should purchase this book. Or are you wondering if this is the right book for you after you made the purchase? I understand this common dilemma. Please stay present and honest with yourself and I think you and I both will like where this journey takes us.

I am writing to you from my point of passion. My passion is living a full life by becoming my best and most authentic self. I'm also tired of watching all the pain that people carry around, causing so many to fall short of living full lives. Help me break this chain. Help me break this cycle one person at a time starting with you.

Who is this man who put that picture on the front cover? Please, allow me to introduce myself. I am a work-in-progress just like you. I have many talents, just like you, and multiple vocations. I am an award-winning wood artist, an organic farmer, a healer, a life coach, an actor in community organizations, and an author. I try to be a human "Being" instead of a human "Doing." I am a seeker of truth and I love what all my training has taught me about life on this planet, including lessons from my livestock and working with my hands.

4.

I have witnessed that life has an ebb and flow, that life works best when there is constant growth, and that when I look with open eyes I see and experience miracles and love.

In this book, we will explore the many Why's and some How's to live life fully. I will offer you a better opportunity to appreciate the true magnitude of the tight grip you have on your baggage, the baggage you have cleverly spun into your life's story.

> *"Our God is too small."*
> *Giordano Bruno*

I may be blunt at times. I have found that sugarcoating life does not work so well.
You may or may not sense a tone of frustration in my writing. The frustration comes from my belief that carrying your past is preventable and fixable.

When I talk about God in this book, I speak of a spiritual God that cannot be used to hustle money, sell fear, fight wars, or meet any other convoluted agenda of mankind. It is difficult for me to define God with our limited language. Perhaps the following incredible true story may help explain how I perceive God,

On March 7, 2012, the world lost a very special man, Lawrence Anthony. Lawrence lived in Africa and was known as the Elephant Whisperer. About the turn of the 21st Century, Lawrence saved a herd of rogue elephants from being exterminated. Years later, when Lawrence died, two different herds of elephants from two different areas made the long trip of over 12 hours to Lawrence's home. They stood outside his house and mourned for two days and then quietly left.

5

I know that the elephants did not read about his passing in the newspaper. This, my friend, is God!

In my healing and coaching practice, I have been truly touched and honored to have witnessed many people expand and grow the lives they came here to live. It is my hope that you will read this book with honesty and with an open-mind. Come walk with me. To YOU.

"The only thing we are ever dealing with is a thought, and a thought can be changed."

Louise Hay

Chapter **0.9**
The "F" word

"The cave you fear to enter holds your treasure."
Joseph Campbell

Why Chapter 0.9 you ask. The fractional number symbolizes that this chapter is a door opening immediately before the nuts and bolts, and maybe even the nails, begin. Please, stay with the journey. I promise we will get to that cover photograph in Chapter One.

I am about to use the four-letter "F" word that disturbs most people. Fear. Have you thought about how big this word is in your life? Fear. Did you ever wonder why God put everything we really want on the other side of fear? Do you figure this was a mistake? Look back at your achievements in life. Did you have to address any fears? Remember the effort it took to get out of your safety zone and face down your fears to reach this goal.

I had the opportunity to overcome a fear before I could even begin to think about writing this book. When I was a junior in high school, my English composition teacher read my essay in class as an example of what not to do. I was hurt and ashamed. He did not reveal to the class who the author was, however, I was sure everyone knew it was me. I could have held on to that pain. I could have accepted my identity as a poor student, rather than as a budding author.

I could have said, "The teacher is right. I give up." Had I done that, you and I would not be having this interaction about this very important topic: LIFE.

Fear does not stop death, unless a Tyrannosaurus Rex is about to grab you! Fear freezes life! Does fear stop you in your tracks, or does it motivate you to keep going, to change and grow? The decisions you make about fear will directly affect the quality of your life. What I have found interesting about fear is that many people think that they are the only ones experiencing fear or that they are the only ones who have a need to hide and disguise their fear. The truth is that everyone has some kind of fear. Some use it as fuel; some use it as a security blanket. Some wake up to find that the security blanket is smothering them and seek help to get past the fear. Some wrap their blanket tighter.

> *"Courage is being scared spitless but saddling up anyway."*
> *John Wayne*

Barbra Streisand is a very well known and talented singer and actor. Barbra suffers from severe stage fright before each performance. She puts her fear to the side and delivers her passion. She delivers what she came here to do. The world would be a lesser place had she given into her fear and not given us her gift.

Please look at all the times in your life that you overcame fear. Many of these would have been when you were very young. If you had not overcome fear as an infant you would still be crawling around in diapers. You see it **can** be done and **you can do it**. The trouble starts when people forget that overcoming fear is a never-ending process. Many people handle their everyday fears but hold on to one or two life-changing fears. They try to live with those fears, keep them stuffed down.

It takes tremendous energy to keep the lid on those impacted feelings, and it is a truly futile effort. You ask these folks to work on releasing those life changers and they give you a look as though you just asked them to untangle a string of Christmas lights.

Now, before you read another word, please, write down two fears that you still allow to smother your life. While you read this book, keep asking yourself, "Do these two fears really feel that good to me now? Are they pretty much harmless all wrapped up and stuffed down in that blanket?"

What is the most common driving force behind fear? CHANGE! Now I have gone and used another big word.

We often convince ourselves that we are comfortable with keeping our painful past. We may not exactly like where we are, but we don't know about changing our lives. We don't know what is behind door number two. It would be easier to stay right where we are, wrapped in that blanket of fear. "Can't I just settle for the path of least resistance?"

I also invite you, while you read, to look at this scary word: Change. *Fear* and *change*. These two words have stopped so many lives. In fact, they often join forces to create a fear *of* change. Do you want to allow a mere ten letters of the alphabet to stand between your current situation and the real you?

Before you get to Chapter One, I have listed below the all the great people throughout history who have not conquered fear and change.

The list :

Wow! What a list! Fear is simply a chosen feeling that some of us give too much power. If you focus on your fear, it will grow. We are what we focus on. Before you turn the page, please, for the short time it takes to read this book, switch the way you use fear to using fear as a fuel. Perhaps a better way to say it is to have fear work for you rather than have it stop your progress. Remember that fear is ever-present, so use it instead of allowing it to use you. If using fear as fuel is a new concept to you try this approach. The above mentioned T-Rex is about to grab you, you can choose one of two options, allow fear to freeze you in your tracks or use it as fuel to run faster then the guy next to you. Become aware of what will happen if you keep using fear as a security blanket.

With that said, have a blast!

"I am not a teacher, but an awakener".

Robert Frost

Chapter **1**
BANG!

"He who opens a door to learning closes a prison."
Victor Hugo

Yes, that is my hand, my thumb and my nail on the front cover. On March 13, 2012, I shot my thumb with a sixteen penny framing nail. This was my first and last attempt at Do-It-Yourself body piercing! Now, if you want to slow down a job and take a break, one way is to shoot yourself with a nail gun. If you want to speed up your thought process, shoot yourself with a nail gun. I promise it will yield both results.

I do, however, believe there are safer and more productive ways to achieve those two goals. Stop and think about the power and speed that an air gun needs to shoot nails through three inches of wood. I know I did. Think about a sixteen-penny nail not exactly being a surgical instrument. I was working with my cousin Tom on an old farmhouse remodel when I got sloppy with the nail gun and BANG! It happened fast.

The play-by-play looked like this. I had the gun in my left hand (I am right-handed) holding it upside down trying to nail a header into place. This being a remodel job meant that I had to do odd angles and hold my mouth just right to get the new work installed into the existing structure. My right hand was holding the header when I pulled the trigger. BANG! Instant pain.

11

I dropped the gun, screaming. I believe I also said, "OH GOSH DARN!" I was reluctant to look at my thumb. Tom ran over to see it. A man from another crew ran up the stairs to see if he could help. My thoughts started racing. Will my thumb be permanently damaged? How long will it take to heal? I don't have time to nurse a thumb back to health. Do I need to go to the emergency room? Can we pull it out? The worker who had run up the stairs, ran back downstairs for extraction tools and came back with a large set of lineman's pliers. By this time my hand was shaking and seeing him with those huge pliers was not a warm, fuzzy feeling. Trust me.

I had some decisions to make. Pull it or leave it in? Tom quickly assessed the situation. He thought he could pull it without a doctor's help. Decisions, decisions. I still had to make mine. If I went to the doctor, I would pretty well be turning my thumb over to professionals, meaning "Here, you take care of my problem for me." I would get a shot to kill the pain, some antibiotics, a tetanus shot, and a prescription for pain medication at home. I would probably be told to take it easy for a while and schedule a follow-up appointment if needed. What if it hurt when Tom pulled it out? What if I chose to leave the nail in?

What? You say leave a 3.25" long nail in your thumb? Leave a nail in your dominant hand's thumb, the most important digit you have? Well, you have to admit it was a choice. I was still walking, talking, and functioning with it in my thumb. My thumb was not bleeding with the nail in there. If I pulled it, it would certainly hurt and bleed -- who knows how much?

The choices and decisions that I made on that day would affect the rest of my life. Of course, a nail in my thumb may qualify as a big decision, but I find that all the choices and decisions we all make every day affect the rest of our lives.

To pull it or not? We shall see.

"Don't wait for extraordinary opportunities.
Seize common occasions and make them great. Weak men wait for opportunities; strong men make them."

Orison Swett Marden

CHAPTER **2**

YEAH, YEAH, YEAH!

"Live out of your imagination, not your history."

Stephen Covey

Yes, I know what you are saying, "Well, he certainly pulled the nail." Maybe you said, "I know it would not be pain-free or easy to pull, but the nail has to come out!"

Well, this is where your contribution becomes critical in this book. What is your nail to pull? What is your emotional issue or wound that you said, "No, just leave it in; I will deal with it. I don't want to have any issues." Please read those last few sentences again, and give them some time to provoke reflection. This is your chance to drop your old pattern of operating from a defensive position, a fearful position. You have the illusion that the defensive pattern you keep serves you. I promise you, that maintaining a defensive stance, staying on guard, has exhausted you! While reading this book you will get many invitations to drop the defense and elevate to offense. If you accept the invitation now you will harvest much more from this book. You see while I was writing this book I found nails I did not know I still had. The fact is we all have issues. No one grows up without a wound or gift, something that does not belong to him or her. That's right. I said, "Does not belong to him or her." You may not believe this yet; however, it is a critical point that you will come to understand soon, and it will make a huge difference. I will discuss this in more detail later in the book.

14

This is where many of you will say, "Yeah, yeah, yeah. I have heard this before -- self-growth, self-improvement, yeah, yeah, yeah." Allow me to take a stab at seeing if I know you. Let me know how close I get.

You have doubts and fears. Most of the time the self-talk that you speak is degrading to yourself. In fact, at times it is bad enough that if you had a friend say the same things to you, they would be a friend no more. You think you are your past. You think you are your behavior. You operate from a belief that something is wrong with you. You compare yourself to others and they usually win. You compare yourself to others and you always win. You feel trapped in a body you don't like. You want, for the most part, to go unnoticed and not make any waves. You enjoy your unchanging world, the status quo that you have made to your liking.

You deny your greatness, your inner beauty. You ask yourself over and over "what will people think?" You probably think you are a human being at times having a spiritual experience, rather than a spiritual being having a human experience. You don't accept compliments well. You may want to improve certain areas of your life, but who has the time? You may even believe that you are the job that you have. You may have thoughts that "if only people really knew about me, they would reject me." You may have a nagging feeling that something is missing.

There. How close am I? Too close for comfort?

I invite you to say **YES, YES, YES,** *I choose freedom from the above list! I long for a nail-free life! I embrace freedom from self-talk that steals from my soul!* All of this is closer than you think. Actually, most of it is only a thought or two away. So YEA, jump in, and let's get to work.

15

"The mind is not a vessel to be filled, but a fire to be lit."
Plutarch

I am a former building mover. I became a self-taught building mover and formed Graham's Building Movers. We placed steel beams and dollies under intact houses and barns, then transported them down the road or across fields. Moving buildings does not come with a manual or set of instructions; therefore, there were many opportunities for me to overcome obstacles. It is an occupation that will test the strength of one's emotional fitness, believe me. There were many times that fear could have stopped me. If that had happened, I would not have moved one single building. Trust me, fear was ever present. I chose to step up and seize the opportunity to grow stronger.

Generations of movers before me used wood timbers instead of steel beams to support structures. Those earlier contractors picked mostly elm timber, and specifically elm trees that grew on the outside edge of the woods. Movers needed reliable timbers capable of handling tough jobs. Those trees on the outside edge of the woods had grown strong and tough enduring more stress from wind and storms through the years than the interior trees.

Nature offers another glimpse at the power of growth. We have all seen plants grow in the cracks of driveways and sidewalks. This is what plants are here to do. Grow and not give up, no matter the conditions. Take a cutting off the top of that plant and watch what it does. Does it give up and die or does it branch out and keep growing?

The same energy that flows through that plant in the sidewalk flows through us. We humans are the only ones with a brain smart enough to <u>not</u> get the message. If we look we will find that every time God asks His creatures to step up and gain strength, it is always possible. Your winds and storms of life will make you stronger and tougher if you deal with and transform them, instead of hiding from them. When we accept the invitation to grow, we get stronger. When we choose to reject the invitation, we get weaker.

Well, I ask, what is our purpose in life? Why are we here? What did we come to earth to do? Did we come here to simply suffer and die? Do we intend to shuffle along and let our past wear us down to a mediocre or wasted life? Why is this book in your hands? Were we brought to this earth, this life, to have our un-pulled nails snag on things to fester and consume our lives?

> *"There are two great days in a person's life – the*
> *day we were born and the day we find out why."*
> *William Barclay*

Or were we brought here to embrace challenges (i.e. embrace a full life) and be all the stronger for it? Were you brought here to display the divine spark of God in a unique way that only you can do? Do caterpillars know more than we do about the power of change?

What do people say when they hear about a near-death experience? It's often something similar to this: "Wow, they were lucky. God must not be done with them yet. They must have something left to complete here on earth." The tragedy of such statements is that the people making them often believe that the person who just dodged death is the only one with a mission here.

17

Don't we all have a mission that is just as important? If we are still breathing, then we have a mission to complete!

Alternatively, we might say, "I'll bet he looks at life differently from now on." Do you really want or need that kind of a wakeup call about your life? Is it so hard to believe that you can simply make a choice to look at your life differently from now on?

My purpose in writing this book is to give you a new perspective on your nail. This is a graphic example that you can use to live your full life and complete your mission, free from the past, and free from your nail.

I invite you to drop your old story, drop your defenses, and live with Emotional Freedom/Fitness. Stop saying to yourself, "This is where I am -- stuck!" To me being stuck is having a 200-ton structure loaded on beams and dollies and finding a soft spot in the ground that can't support it.. The only thing you are stuck in is a feeling or a belief. Being stuck in either soft ground or in a belief is solvable. Both can be changed.

What is Emotional Freedom/Fitness? It is living your truth, not someone else's. It is living in the present and fulfilling your needs in positive ways. It is not renting space in your head to others. It is living with a sense of wonder, with an open mind, and embracing self-growth. You might find it helpful to think of this idea with the condensed definition of Emotional Freedom/Fitness - living your truth through self-growth.

"Nothing changes until you do."
Mike Robbins

Today's recipe
Self-growth

Ingredients
Copious amounts of fresh curiosity
Three pounds of new rituals
Five buckets of freshly picked meanings
Frosting = new challenges

Directions
First make sure your countertop is cleansed thoroughly
from all past recipes.
Now, take this curiosity and simmer it at low heat, enjoy the
aroma. Allow it to fill everything. Make sure you always stay
in curious and never go to furious.
Next add one pound of news rituals, stir often. Then, add
the freshly picked meanings. These are the glue, so chose
only the best.
Bake this at extreme life. For 60 seconds every minute.
Consume with liberal amounts of frosting, i.e. New
Challenges.

CHAPTER **3**

CHEATING WILL NOT WORK

"We cannot solve our problems with the same thinking we used when we created them"
Albert Einstein

Now back to my decision: my nail. What if I cheated? What if I left the nail in and just kept my right hand out of all work? What if I only chose tasks that I could use the remaining healthy, nail-free digits on that hand? How about I cut the nail on each side of my thumb and leave the middle section in? I know I could just take pain medication for the rest of my life. What if I said, "I will pull it later?"

So what kind of a face did you just make relating to leaving the nail in? My bet is it looked a lot like the face you make when you walk into spider web, and get it plastered on your face.

Here is a long but incomplete list. I have attempted to provide all the options that we humans choose to avoid growth and leave the nail in our lives. Look through this list and pick your poison.

I could pull my nail or I could...

START SMOKING
OVEREAT
NEVER LEAVE MY HOUSE
BECOME ALCOHOLIC

GAIN WEIGHT
ABUSE PRESCRIPTION DRUGS
GET HOOKED ON ILLEGAL DRUGS
ABUSE FAMILY MEMBERS
BECOME AN OUTLAW
DEVELOP A TICK OR ITCH THAT WON'T STOP
STUTTER
NOT ALLOW JOY
NOT ALLOW ANGER (Yes, sometimes anger is
appropriate.)
NOT ALLOW HAPPINESS
NOT ALLOW LAUGHTER
PICK MY SKIN
BITE MY FINGERNAILS
HOARD THINGS
SHUT DOWN CREATIVITY
WON'T HAVE SEX
WON'T ALLOW SEXUAL JOY
CLEAN MY HOUSE OVER AND OVER
TRUST NO ONE
ADOPT RACISM
HATE MEN
REFUSE TO TRY NEW THINGS
HATE WOMEN
REFUSE TO TAKE CHANCES
HATE MYSELF
HATE OTHERS
BLAME OTHERS
JUDGE EVERYTHING AS BAD
SHUT PEOPLE OUT
DECIDE I CAN'T ACHIEVE
DECIDE MONEY IS BAD
USE THE PROBLEM TO GET ATTENTION
BECOME A HERMIT
GET DEPRESSED
WORK ALL THE TIME

REFUSE TO SMILE
USE IT TO HOLD ME BACK
USE IT TO PRETEND I FEEL SECURE
ADOPT AN EATING DISORDER
MAKE IT MY LIFE STORY
COMMIT SUICIDE

I apologize if I missed your choice of distraction.

The stories we create about our wound are actually the distraction we use to hide from our true potential. This potential-killing deceptive script keeps us from the life we were meant to live! It becomes the filter that we use to view all of our lives. This filter forces us to confuse perception with reality. Imagine how this fictional script affects our interaction with others and our own self-image.

I was once invited to give a talk about releasing emotional baggage at a women's networking group. The organizer of the group and I were talking over details a couple of days before the event when I noticed that she kept rubbing and fidgeting with her thumb. I looked closer and saw the thumb was rubbed red raw from constant friction. I asked if that thumb issue and the emotional driver behind it was something that she would like to release. She immediately said no and chose the route that many take, "I would rather have this known problem than look at what is on the other side of the freedom curtain!" She knew what my presentation was about and she still chose to have a sore thumb for the rest of her life!

People often are not open and honest with others about who they are because they are using their false script. If one is not careful all they present to the world is their past their pain.

This is an example of the statement from Chapter Two, the "self-talk that steals from me." This self-talk is ever so quiet but ever so present, which is how it takes over by default. This script is written with you as a victim trying to escape the past. This outdated script thrives on limits and lies. You may as well tell people you enjoy going to the Bureau of Motor Vehicles.

The good news is that you are not your worst old memories, even though you don't believe it yet. Now grab on tight because I am going to say it. What you are is pure love energy! Did you hear that? Yes, I went there. You come from love and will return to love. Many of us forget this while we walk on this planet. When those of you who have forgotten this are reminded, you will immediately argue for your limitations. You will offer your past as your truth. Now, allow that to stir inside you for a while.

"When you are reminded or simply remember that there is more to you than meets the eye... give yourself that gift of reconnecting to yourself and to Source Own again who you are and what you came here to do. It will strengthen your flow, it will raise your resonance, and it will make all of your creations easier and more elegant. Because it is true. You are a piece of God. And you are loved. Deeply, unequivocally, unconditionally loved."
        Boni Lonnsburry

We all try to cheat life at times and take the easy way. The following is my story of trying to cheat as an eight-year-old boy. I hope you will see what I have learned, that life will not be cheated.

When I was eight years old I broke my left femur twice - once in a sledding accident, and the second time while in traction in the hospital.

After eight weeks in traction and eight weeks at home in a half body cast, I was released to start walking with crutches. Do you suppose there was any fear attached to this new task? Yes, there was so I started cheating. I walked around on my crutches with my left leg slightly bent so as to not allow it to touch the floor, let alone bear any weight. This cheating and self-protection caused my left leg and knee joint to freeze at about a twelve-degree angle.

The doctor ordered my father to work on my leg every night after work. While I lay on my back my father would grab my left heel in one hand and push down on my knee with his other hand. We did this until my knee became flexible. Trust me this was not fun! I had nightmares that my dad would push too hard and break my knee backwards. This is a classic example of what trying to cheat got me, additional problems to fix on top of the original problem! The hidden blessing was the opportunity to learn this valuable lesson at such a young age.

I am a firm believer that you incarnated into this lifetime to expand the divine spark inside of you. To grow your soul to display the God within you as only you can. Do not argue for your limitations. I know some of you went there instantly. This is doable. End of story!

Now, God knows what She is doing and presents to us exactly what we need to do to achieve our greatest potential. Usually we see what God gives us as a problem. If you try to get around the problem and cheat life, it will simmer and boil inside you and eventually boil over into a giant problem.

I do not mean to say that God is testing us. God is cajoling you to expand and grow. If you are not growing you are dying. We have all seen people who have died inside long before they are buried.

Norman Cousins, author of *Anatomy of an Illness*, said, "Death is not the greatest loss; the greatest loss is what dies inside of us while we are alive." Some people choose to never get the message and they cheat all the way to their grave.

I am reminded of my father who was 90-years-old when he died. My father was not valued as a youth. His way to handle that rejection was to assign a meaning that he was not good enough. He had very low self-esteem and went through life seeking outside approval for everything he did. Everyone needs approval from others; however, it is not healthy when outside approval is one's only source of approval. My father could be owned with a compliment (especially one from a woman) and he could be destroyed with criticism.

Because of his dependence, he satisfied his need for significance by thinking he had to be married, which was yet another source for outside approval. My mother died too young -- in middle age. He remarried at 80-years-old and the second wife died shortly after that. Marriage is a fine arrangement, but if you enter it to get your needs met you are missing what it is all about. He, like many, would rather have a troop of Howler monkeys move in next to him than to change and grow.

My father spent the last year and a half of his life in an assisted living facility. He was still relying solely on outside validation. Because of that dependence, he asked three women to marry him after only knowing them for a couple of weeks.

Do you want to keep trying to cheat life and end up dealing with your nail at the age of 90? Do you and I live our lives as a warning or an example? Everyone dies but not everyone lives.

"Nothing is more damaging than to do something that you believe is wrong."
Abraham / Esther Hicks

CHAPTER **4**
YES, BUT

> *"The lust for comfort, that stealthy thing that enters the house as a guest, and then becomes a host, and then a master."*
>
> *Khalil Gibran*

How often do we say *Yes, But* in our lives? How often do we convey with our self-talk *Yes, But* in our lives. Your nail makes you use the *Yes, But* language. Allow me to give you a few examples, maybe the top five of what I have seen through my years.

1. Question: You do know that smoking is bad for you, don't you?
Answer: *Yes, But* I do not think I was loved enough as a child, so I smoke.

2. Question: Do you know that if you released weight you would feel better?
Answer: *Yes, But* I was sexually abused as a child, therefore I need to put on extra weight as protection.

3. Question: Why don't you get out there and have some fun, dance and enjoy life?
Answer: *Yes, But* I can't sing and dance. I was shamed as a youth.

4. Question: Why are you mad at everything? Wouldn't joy be a better way?
Answer: *Yes, But* I can't find joy I was told not to display that emotion as a child.

5. Question: You do know that to grow you will have to leave your comfort zone don't you?
Answer: *Yes, But* I was raised by an alcoholic father. I can't do that.
Yes, But I would rather get an unneeded root canal than look at my emotional baggage!

We have all heard the quote from Albert Einstein: "Insanity is doing the same thing over and over and expecting different results." How many of us use our *Yes, Buts* not in any way to expect different results, but to insure the same result? "No thanks, just give me the same results." To expect different results means you have to look at your relationship to change. Is it insane to not understand that it is impossible for life to stay the same?

I invite you to look at how much energy you invest trying to stay the same in an ever changing world. If you are honest with yourself you will see the constant adjustments it takes to attempt to fool the system. The only thing that is constant is change.

The sample questions and answers above are only five samples that are as extensive as the human spirit. If you are not careful, they will smother your spirit. We must be vigilant not to live with the illusion that our *Yes, Buts* keep us safe. Every *Yes, But* we use is stealing our potential for excellence. Every *Yes, But* is that self-talk that steals from us, lies to us.

I have seen far too many *Yes, Buts* keep people in their comfort zones. I invite you to ask yourself, "Is my comfort zone killing me?" For many people, the answer is yes.

Some people will use a *Yes,But* that is formed from a label. We must be very careful about what labels we accept for ourselves. Look at the label of " I am claustrophobic." In my opinion the only thing different between a claustrophobic person and a non-claustrophobic person is the thought process upon entering smaller spaces. In other words are people a label or are they a person that spends too much time in fearful thinking.

I offer you this challenge as you read the rest of this book. If you catch yourself saying *Yes, But*, I challenge you to stand on one leg until you can restate your excuse(s) in a positive manner.

"One can choose to go back toward safety or forward toward growth. Growth must be chosen again and again. Fear must be overcome again and again."
Abraham Maslow

Life in your comfort zone.

"Why do you stay in prison when the door is so wide open?"
Rumi

This is what it looks life outside your comfort zone, or as Neale Donald Walsch says, "Life begins at the edge of your comfort zone."

Probably the biggest *Yes, But* that I hear from clients is, **Yes** I would love to do that, (fill in the blank) **But** those other people doing great things have special skills and have an inner drive that I do not.

Did you know that the Cirque du Soleil performers did not grow up in the acrobatic world? They were regular civilians trained to perform these unbelievable feats. They were selected not for already having special acrobatic talent, but because they chose to be aggressive students who took well to training. They were able to make dramatic changes quickly with the help of outstanding coaches.

This begs a very important question. Which comes first -- an inner drive or overcoming challenges? Does the taste of victory over a problem instantly condition a need for more, thereby giving us inner drive? We often think people at the top of their field have a charmed life while we are doomed to live a life of obstacles and difficulty. The singer or athlete who performs for us makes it look so easy that we forget the old 10,000 hour rule: to achieve mastery at something you need to put in 10,000 hours of quality time.

How many people have far more than 10,000 hours in creating a life they are not happy with. The special skill they excel at is stuffing past pain and hiding their uniqueness.

No one learns to play Wimbledon champion tennis or Masters champion golf in a weekend. Tiger Woods was swinging a golf club at age two. We don't see the sacrifices these high-achievers make. They sacrifice their limiting beliefs for true human potential. If truth were known, those high performers, those other people, have had to pull many nails out of their lives. Those high-achievers continue to pull and push and grow.

All they possess that you don't is a set of strategies to get where they want to go and a very clear and powerful end target.

"The wound is the place where the Light enters you."
                                                Rumi

You see, everybody has a nail -- no one gets out unscathed. Everyone has some wound or gift given to him or her. This wound or gift is by design, given by a higher power. Without a gift, without a struggle, what could any of us overcome?

I am reminded of the butterfly story. A woman discovers a cocoon on a plant in her garden. She looks closer and notices that it has a small wiggle to it. She watches closely and spots a wing on the right side start to break free from the cocoon. She watches with great interest as the wing pushes and strains against the barrier. Finally it pops out and opens up for the drying process. She then looks to the left side and can see the start of the left wing pushing. She has a big heart so she decides to help, so she runs to get some small scissors. She hurries back, makes a few small cuts in the cocoon, and out pops the left wing much faster. The wing was out but it did not open for the drying process, it just hung there. See, the left wing never had the opportunity to struggle and build the muscle to open. The butterfly never flew. The caterpillar never soared as a butterfly because it did not complete the full struggle of the change process. The butterfly was forced into another life of crawling.

How many of us use our fears, or our *Yes, Buts* as scissors and eliminate our chance of flying? When I was a youth, some television shows still had some redeeming values.

I remember picking up a quote from a western character named Lucas McCain star of *The Rifleman* that I still use today. "Nothing ventured, nothing gained."

We need to have skin in the game, something to live for. This something is your big WHY. There is a yearning inside of you. Do not deny this for inside that yearning lies your life.

Will you be the next Michael Jordan if you stop using your *Yes, But*? Okay, most of us will not grow to over 6 ½ feet tall and develop that amazing basketball talent. However, I promise that if you release your *Yes, Buts* you will become the Michael Jordan of your specialty. The invitation is to become your best and your most authentic self. What is it God blessed you with?

Yes, I know some of you have pulled your *Yes, But* out two to three sentences ago. That *Yes, But* may have sounded like this: *Yes, But* what they went through is not as bad as what I went through. So, are you standing on one leg? Are you working to put a positive spin on that excuse?

Please, stay with me, I have heard stories of the living hell that people have gone through. However, we get to assign the meaning to every event in our own lives. The meaning we assign to any event is the only thing we can actually control. The event itself is ancient history -- it cannot be changed. Do our meanings lift us up or knock us down? That is up to each individual every time.

Perhaps the people we admire for doing great things assigned meaning in their lives to use obstacles as stepping-stones to reach goals instead of settling for less. Is it possible that those people achieving great feats have a goal rooted in excellence instead of a goal rooted in comfort?

Maybe we actually admire them just for being true to why they came here? Perhaps they recognized, honored, and focused on their big WHY and making that big dream come true?

> *"It is far better to set a high goal and miss,*
> *than to set a low goal and hit it."*
> *Les Brown.*

While your goals may be unstated or vague, trust me, they are still goals. We all have goals. Some are just way more juicy!

> *"We're all faced with great opportunities brilliantly*
> *disguised as insoluble problems."*
> *John Gardner*

If we embraced Gardner's statement just imagine how that would help, adding uplifting meanings to our lives. Is there truly a difference between a small and a big problem? Is the only difference how much mental anguish we assign to a problem? If people are not careful they will label a problem as big, and therefore unsolvable. I use in my life a slightly different version of John Gardner's quote -- *The bigger the problem, the greater the opportunity.* If people want to label a problem as big, look at the opportunity they have. This means God knew they were big enough to handle the gift chosen for them. So, that also means that if they reach deep enough they will find the ability to rise to the big opportunity.

We all admire a powerful human spirit story when a person overcomes some huge obstacle, faces the odds and wins. Look at the attraction to the Paralympic Games where people achieve greatness despite missing limbs.

Do these athletes assign a positive or negative meaning to the challenge given to them? It would be very easy for these people to say, "A wheelchair is what I need for the rest of my life, and so I must accept that I cannot achieve great things." And some of you right now are saying *Yes, But* they have an inner drive that I do not have. Back to my previous statement, this is where we have to have skin in the game. Take a chance. Christopher Columbus did! Something to live for as well as something we would die for. Your yearning is calling.

I have had the chance to witness the human spirit in action several times. Here are two of my favorite stories.

Have you heard of Nick Vujicic? If not, look him up online. He was born with no arms and no legs. Despite this lack of limbs Nick, is an inspirational public speaker and an athlete in his own right. Nick should be an inspiration to all of us. He is running circles around many of us by living his life, his fantastic life. Nick took the lemons that life handed him and made lemonade, lemon pie, and lemon cake, and he still has some left to sprinkle on you and me. Thank you, Nick, for displaying your divine spark to my world.

A few years ago, I worked with a man for two days on a construction site. Due to a farming accident, he was missing both hands, but he did not let that slow him down. He had prosthetic hands and did not miss a lick of work or a lick of healthy mental attitude. These two powerful men did not dwell on and count their liabilities. They used all of the blessings they were given at birth.

When was the last time you counted your blessings? You see as my friend Tony Robbins says, "Change is never about ability, it is about a motivation."

Remember I said the only difference between a small problem and a big problem is how much mental anguish we assign to it? Just for argument's sake, let's assign degrees of wounds. Let us label them small problems and big problems. Perhaps small problems could be not enough love or positive attention, some shame issues, parental divorce, and the like. I have seen these lead to several issues, such as the following:

- weight gain,
- addictions,
- nail biting,
- stuttering,
- low self-esteem,
- anger,
- and so forth

All of these "small problems" can and need to be transformed. I have also seen these so-called small problems lead to greatness and excellence.

Big problems could be sex abuse, physical beatings, alcoholic parents, etc. I've seen these big problems lead to several issues, such as the following:

- weight gain,
- addictions,
- nail biting,
- stuttering,
- low self-esteem,
- anger,
- and so forth.

These big problems can and need to be transformed as well. In fact, did you notice that both small and big problems often lead to the same issues? I have also seen so-called big problems lead to greatness and excellence.

Some small problems are not always as clear, so we often wonder and search for why life is not working the way we thought it would. The absence of abuse denies us a defining moment. One advantage of a big problem is that most of the time we know what the event was. We know what past traumatic event is haunting us.

"Fear of the Devil is one way of doubting God."
Khalil Gibran

Yes, But, you may say, it was their fault that they did that to me. Here we go again. I lost some of you in your *Yes, But* it was their fault! If only they had not done this to me. Try carrying that with you for the rest of your life. Make sure you tell St. Peter at the Pearly Gates about your strife. Now don't get me wrong, God will not judge you if you carry this to the Pearly Gates. Many institutions have stayed alive by being the middleman and selling fear that God is a judging entity. Nothing could be further from the truth! How could judgment possibly come from a source that is love only.

"I would rather have my mind opened by wonder
than closed by a belief."
Gerry Spence

We don't have to do any of this any more than the baby has to learn to walk. We **get** to do this! If a baby never learned to walk she could survive. Ask yourself do you want to survive or live? Sure the baby thinks she has to walk. The baby thinks walking is hard to learn at first. However, the baby keeps trying and ultimately will run with joy. Perhaps babies have not learned yet from emotional wounds to hold themselves back. Maybe babies still have a strong connection to the divine spark inside them. Stop and ask yourself this: do you want to simply survive or run with joy?

Many times I ask my clients, what if this "bad event" never happened? What would your life look like? Somewhere in their psyche they are saying if only this or that did not happen. "If only...," yes my life would have been how I wanted it.

Please, look at this closely. One "bad" event prevented your greatness? Who made that decision? There are three forms of blame. Blame someone else, blame an event, or blame yourself. All three forms of blame are useless to the person who wants Emotional Freedom/Fitness. Life happens for you, not to you!

So how do these wounds happen? Who are the perpetrators? These wounds can happen any time any place. In my experience, the top three perpetrators are the well-loved institutions of family, schools and organized religion. When we are in our formative years we spend about 100% of our time with our family where we often pick up beliefs and habits that belong to someone else. We often pick up behaviors simply by observing the behaviors that our parents or the adults around us display. The modeling my father showed me about how to honor one's wife was something I wish I had not learned. I learned to try to only get my needs met, not value my wife's needs. This resulted in a compromised relationship. I am grateful my wife and I survived my learned behavior long enough for me to unlearn it. This "learned" behavior is a classic example of my accepting another's' truth as my own without any awareness that I did it.

39

The school years can be wounding in so many different ways. In school, many of us were trained to compare our grades to others, to learn that we were a test score. You can be told that you have a learning disability because many times the one-size-fits-all education system does not work.

And, then there is organized religion. All I will say about this is that far too many people find religion, not God in these institutions. Of course, this world is filled with other perpetrators who cause emotional wounds: violence, abuse, and bad bosses at work, ad infinitum.

> " Rather than placing a label on yourself such
> as Christian, Jew Muslim, Buddhist, or
> whatever, instead make a commitment to be
> Christ-like, God-like, Buddha-like and
> Mohammed-like."
> Wayne Dyer

What if a person is stuck on an idea that was just a misunderstanding? We have all seen where communication breaks down because a person perhaps misses one word. Communication can be very tricky between two people. Changing just which word is emphasized in a sentence can change the whole meaning. Read the following three sentences and watch for the bold emphasized word.

- **I** did not say he stole the money.
- I did not say **he** stole the money.
- I did not say he **stole** the money.

I remember an example of this that I witnessed. I once observed two men talking. I knew what each one was saying but they missed something in the heat of the conversation -- they were one word off.

Pete was talking about small trailers behind motorcycles. Charlie was talking about towing a motorcycle behind a car.

The miscommunication resulted in Pete thinking that Charlie was saying that motorcycles had bumpers. What if you are running your life as a victim over a one-word misunderstanding?

What if you are living your life from the miscommunication that you have with yourself? That negative self-talk that is all too happy to steal from you. You think, "This is who I am. I am powerless." The idea that "I am not good enough" may have come from a simple miscommunication and now you think you need bumpers to get through life.

Whatever the source of the wound is, we get to transform the problem into opportunity! It is our responsibility to say, "This, I will not own. This, I will not carry. This, I will not allow to darken my life one more second."

The next responsibility we have is to take action based on those declarations. "*Yes, But* I can't go back and relive all that stuff, it will kill me." When I work with people I don't ask them to relive the nail. Going back and immersing yourself in the past trauma will not change the event. The only thing we can change is what meaning we assign the event now. We only have control of what is inside of us. I ask my clients to take action and I help them assign new meaning to their nails.

We all know the saying -- "It's not what happens to you, it is what you do with what happens to you that defines you." Maybe it's time to take that statement to heart and not just skim over it. Many clients may try to escape the opportunity in the present by reliving the past during each session. This pattern needs to broken quickly.

41

A good coach keeps clients looking forward, uncovering creative resources they already possess. The time I spend with each client may be short - a few sessions - or longer if needed. The amount of time spent is based on each individual client's needs and his or her progress.

What we possess is by far greater than what our limited egos allow us to believe. Some people are forced to find their greatness through tragic events.

We all have heard stories of great feats of strength, courage, and will where people were placed in physically tragic events, perhaps even in their own families. The people in those stories rose to the occasion, met the challenge, and formed a formidable memory of personal strength and power, as well as an inspiring example of reaching one's full potential.

Aaron Ralston is great example of what we can do when we are put in a bad spot. Aaron wrote *Between a Rock and a Hard Place,* then Hollywood made a movie based on his story. In case you don't know Aaron's story, here is a very quick recap.

Aaron was hiking alone through Blue John Canyon in Utah when a boulder shifted and pinned his arm against a canyon wall. The condensed story is after six days Aaron amputated his own arm so he could escape to find help. We don't have to be put in life threatening spots to find the depth of our will. Look at sports history and you find many examples where the underdog dug deep inside to triumph over their obstacles and win the impossible game.

I believe most of the people in these tragic events were surprised at what they found inside of themselves, exactly when they needed it most.

Now, we on the sidelines say to ourselves, "No, I don't have it in me." This lowball assumption is premature because no one really knows their own power until the opportunity for it arises. Of course, this also applies to everyday challenges, too.

Some people find their inner power by constantly pushing their own envelope, without needing a traumatic event to reach deep inside. I find it easier to choose the challenge rather than have life force an emergency on me to bring out my best.

Remember, in the preface of this book, I described my friend talking about me becoming an author, and I always sold myself short. "I don't have the skills to write a book." My English teacher reinforced that truth for me. Apparently, life ignored my little comfort-zone limitations and knocked at the door hard enough to shake me out of my illusion.

There are many ways to choose a challenge, such as mountain climbing, learning a new language or a new musical instrument, skydiving, exceptional community service, and many more. The point is to do something different, to answer the call or the yearning you have inside. Take one step outside your comfort zone and watch what happens. Stop selling yourself short. Trust life. We all possess resources far beyond our old patterns of weak self-talk. Is your comfort zone expanding or staying stagnant?

The invitation behind all of this talk about challenge is that we need to operate from more than what we think we possess. The process of getting to what we really possess does not have to be hard.

If only people appreciated the healing power inside of them. If we would release the illusion that we are fragile, oh, the places we could go. With Emotional Freedom/Fitness it is easier to eat right, think right, focus right, and avoid disease. I have a strong belief that you don't get a headache from lack of aspirin in your body.

As we are nearing the end of chapter 4 (or nearly 1/3 of the way through the book), take a look at the two fears you wrote down in chapter 1. Make a note of how you feel now, please. It's important to review progress..

"Who am I to be brilliant, gorgeous, talented, fabulous? Actually, who are you not to be? You are a child of God. We are all meant to shine, as children do. We were born to manifest the glory of God that is within us. As we are liberated from our fear, our presence automatically liberates others."
Marianne Williamson

Today's recipe
Loving life

Ingredients
24 cups of love
12 cups of laughter
48 deep breaths
One trip to the scrap yard

Directions
Gather up all the old rusty nails lying about or interfering with your life.
Take those nails to the scrap yard and cash them in for more life.
Add one cup of love to your life every hour, blend in ½ cup of laughter every hour and add 3 deep breaths each hour and be in awe of what those breaths do.
Now bake this at pure ecstasy for life.
Enjoy this hot and maybe sprinkle with some wonder and awe dust on top.

CHAPTER **5**

WHY BOTHER?

> *"Life is difficult. The sooner we realize that the easier it gets."*
> *Scott Peck*

Sadly, many people think *Why bother?* when someone mentions eliminating old wounds.

So, I ask you, is it possible that if I leave the nail in, it could fester and lead to far bigger health issues, such as cancer, blood poisoning, or range of motion loss?

I would argue that it's not only possible, but highly probable. I would make the same argument regarding emotional wounds. So, *Why bother?*

Here's a few answers to the question *Why Bother*:

1. You are not designed to carry any baggage from your past!
2. You incarnated here to transform problems into opportunities.
3. Staying stuck in the past will directly affect everyone who has a close relationship with you.
4. The pain will increase and your distraction of choice will not work to numb the pain if you stay stuck.

5. Changing and growing will increase your joy and decrease your need for coping mechanisms.
6. This is important and all very doable.
7. If you don't grow I promise that someday you will wish you had.
8. Deep inside you there is a yearning that deserves to be heard.

"The unexamined life is not worth living"
Socrates

The answer to *Why Bother* is to prevent and stop a whole lot of personal pain and suffering. I find that most people who ask *Why Bother* are not sick enough yet. The nail they have not pulled has not festered enough to drive them to action. In September 2007 DR. Mercola from Chicago talked in his newsletter about a study by a German doctor, Dr. Ryke Hamer. Doctor Hamer operates under the premise that every disease, even cancer, originates from an unexpected shock experience.

Dr. Hamer reports two phases of disease, 1. A conflict-active phase. 2. A healing phase. If one does not choose to bother with emotional issues they will be stuck in the conflict –active phase. Do we really want to live in a perpetual state of conflict. I believe that nothing good can come from living in conflict. Dr. Mercola went on to say and I quote. "Even the conservative Centers for Disease Control and Prevention (CDC) states that 85 percent of all diseases have an emotional element. And I believe the actual percentage is much higher." We are not designed to carry this stuff around with us. This is my answer to Why Bother.

"The truth about our childhood is stored up in our bodies, and lives in the depths of our souls. Our intellect can be deceived, our feelings can be numbed and manipulated, our perceptions can be shamed and confused, or our bodies tricked with medication. But our soul never forgets. And because we are one, one whole soul in one body, some day, our body will present its bill."

Alice Miller

The following example should help answer *Why Bother*. One cold, rainy Mother's Day I was called to a local hospital to work on a man in his seventies who had stopped eating. He was fully capable of chewing, swallowing, and digesting, but he stopped eating. I introduced myself to him and went to work with him. We found a 30- to 45-year-old wound/gift that his father had given him. In less than an hour of working together, we transformed his thinking and he returned to eating normally. His release and transformation took place in less than one hour. Transformation does not have to be hard; it does not have to take long. This man's transformation required no medication, no side effects, no years of therapy. Now, who among us would not say that it would've been nice to release this about 45 years earlier?

People still ask *Why Bother*? "I was never beaten, raped, molested as a child." Please, remember that no one gets out unscathed. Everyone is shadowing something.

What does shadowing mean? Shadowing something is anything that your ego won't allow in your life. It could be joy, happiness, success, anger, confidence or any number of other emotions. People shadow a feeling because sometime in life they got in trouble for displaying the emotion. Or, perhaps caregivers never displayed certain emotions.

49

At the minimum, the person doing the shadowing may have displayed the feeling and not been encouraged. So they took the light away from this behavior and shadowed it, banished it from their inventory of emotions. A simple example would look like this. Little four-year-old Johnny loves to sing. Johnny sings loud and proud, he is singing in the living room when a parent who had a tough day scolds him so they can hear the news. This makes Johnny shadow his love of song. This miscommunication from the parent can make a child shadow something in one episode or many. Little Johnny assigns a meaning to his singing as bad. Johnny removes that joyous activity from his inventory of activities. Who knows, maybe Johnny grows up and looks to alcohol to fill that void.

> *Nothing has a stronger influence psychologically*
> *on their environment and especially on their children than the*
> *unlived life of the parent.*
> *Carl Jung*

Yes, But, I have tried everything to pull my nail and nothing has worked. I've heard that said more than a few times. Of course, people almost always have a secondary gain they enjoy by keeping their problem.

Think about the two fears you wrote down earlier. Ask yourself, what is the negative result of getting rid of these fears? Do you lose connection, attention, excuses, or something else that you have the illusion that serves you? We all need to see through unfiltered eyes what truly does and does not serve us.

"When you want to do something, you will find a way. When you don't want to do something, you will find an excuse."

Jim Rohn

It is important to make sure you don't switch one problem for another. We've all seen someone quit smoking cigarettes, only to replace that habit with food. The end result is a new problem commonly known as weight gain. The smoker simply switched addictions. He did not address the emotional issues behind the addiction. This is why bariatric surgery fails with so many. We need to learn to fill all our needs in a healthy way. We also need to stop asking doctors to fix our emotional problems with a surgical knife.

Still not convinced why you should bother? I could give you horror stories of crime and deceit in human life when people do not bother to pull their nails. I could give you stories of where keeping a clean spotless house, what most of us would say is harmless, damaged many family members in graphic ways. Damaged human life can come from both ends of the spectrum. I could also refer you back to Chapter 3 and the long list of distractions. That list is a huge answer to Why Bother. However, I will not give you the graphic details of what happens when we forget that we all come from love. All you really need to do to is watch the nightly news for the crime reports. Watch the entertainment news to see what new celebrity is melting down. It will not get any more graphic than that. Perhaps now you may ask when you see these stories of horror -- what nail was festering in that person's soul?

Look at your own life and when you fell short of a dream or goal. Think of a time when you did not treat someone close to you as either of you would have wanted.

51

Reflect on the times in your life when you could have given more but you withheld. Now remember how that felt -- the disappointment, the ache deep inside. This life pattern can be stopped! There is an high chance that you missed the target because of your past. It is the inner voice that steals from you whether it speaks in a small, quiet whisper or a loud, unstoppable roar. You cannot reach the goal because you are still working from limited self-talk. You are presenting only part of yourself to the world, and most of that is probably rooted in scarcity thinking. You see, only 20% of what you want to do is skill and technique. The remaining 80% is pure heart.

I repeat, watch the news, read the newspaper. All the crimes reported -- the rapes, the murders, the lying and cheating, children being molested -- are all the result of people passing their pain on! It is all the result of holding onto the past. The perpetrators of these actions believe that they are their past. Trying to escape from life does not work! Only living life works! This should be all you need to stop asking Why Bother.

"Don't judge him or her. You don't know what they've been through," you might say. After all, who among us has not heard that statement? I do not advocate judging anyone; however, if you had met me 15 to 20 years after I broke my leg and I was still walking on crutches you might wonder about my motives and thought processes. Would the above statement be more productive if it were rephrased? "Don't judge him or her. You don't know what it is that they refused to let go of!" Please, pull your nail and move on to fulfill your mission.

Now, I am going to say *Yes But*. YES there are horrible things that happened to people. BUT there comes a time when we go from victim to volunteer. Yes I said volunteer. If I were still walking on crutches from my broken leg when I was eight years old that makes me a volunteer. If people carry an emotional wound for 50 years, they are volunteers. We also can decide to go from victim to victor. We decide this with the meaning we apply to someone else's unpulled nail. The pain they try to give to us.

"Your pain is the breaking of the shell that encloses
your understanding".
Khalil Gibran

There is a story about a man named Bill, an engineer who dies and goes to heaven. He meets up with St. Peter and he asks, "Who is the best engineer ever?" St. Peter points to a man across the room and says, "Joe over there is the best engineer there ever was." Now Bill happened to know Joe in life, and he says to St. Peter, "Joe wasn't an engineer. He was the town drunk his whole life." And St. Peter answers, "Yes I know, you see somebody in school told Joe he wasn't good at math and Joe believed it."

Did Joe accept someone else's pain as his truth? Did Joe want life to be easy?
If I may be so bold as to rephrase Scott Peck's quote about life from the beginning of this chapter. I would say, *Life is not easy. Stop expecting that it should be.* We incarnated into this world to live our lives. Living life means getting bumps and nails, therefore it is very defeating to say, "Hey, I did not know it would be this hard."

Ask George Dantzig, a professor at Stanford University, what we humans can achieve when we don't know that it can't be done.

53

When George was a graduate student, he was rarely on time to class. On one particular day when he arrived late he saw two math problems on the board and copied them down, he figured they were the homework assignment. George went home and got to work on these very difficult problems. He was surprised at the level of difficulty they possessed. It took him several days to solve them and then he turned them in. Six weeks later his professor excitedly pounded on his door to announce that George had solved both problems that leading mathematicians had so far not been able to solve. The problems were not homework; they were examples of two famous problems yet to be solved.

"To the timid and hesitating everything is impossible because it seems so."
Sir Walter Scott

Everyone we meet will paint a brush stroke on our canvas of life. It is up to each individual to finish the painting and make it into a masterpiece. Your masterpiece can be made by one of two choices. One, you can attempt to paint over your whole canvas with black to hide all the strokes from others. Two, you can blend the good parts of all the strokes from others into your work taking full advantage of what was already there. You are the master of your fate. You are the captain of your soul. Please, make sure you take your own painting with you through life and death.

CHAPTER 6

KEY DECISIONS

"When we are no longer able to change a situation –   we are challenged to change ourselves."
                                    Victor Frankl

What are key decisions? They are the decisions we make when we are under duress. They color our thinking until we seek the truth. They are blanket statements we use to keep ourselves safe. Some common disempowering key decisions include the following:

- The sexual abuse victim sometimes decides sex is bad, I am dirty, I can't display feminine qualities, I need protection, all men are bad, so if I'm overweight I won't be attractive.
- The physical abuse victim often decides I have to be defensive at all times, I have to be quiet, things are generally my fault, I am no good.
- Verbal abuse victims may decide I am responsible for how others feel, others opinions are more important than mine, I need to judge others.

Allow me to illustrate with a simple non life-altering event. Years ago, Nick's family stopped at a small restaurant during a vacation. Nick was served a glass of milk that was curdled. He told both his father and the cook about the spoiled milk. The cook took the milk back to the kitchen, but Nick saw him pour a new glass of milk out of the same carton he had used for the original glass of milk. Nick told his father what he saw, but his father simply told him to, "Shut up and drink the milk."

As he was forced to drink the spoiled milk, Nick unconsciously made the key decision that milk would spoil if it was not constantly refrigerated.

Today Nick is in his 60s and he will not leave milk on the table during a meal. He panics when milk sits on the table, so he serves what he needs and immediately puts the milk back in the refrigerator, even if he or someone else expects to need another serving in a few minutes. Although Nick's childhood experience with spoiled milk was not a life-altering event, it is a good illustration of how a key decision is unconsciously made and how it can become irrational. Now, to be honest, Nick uses a fair amount humor in his life and is not afraid to add some theatrics when I see him deal with his milk issue.

Many of us have a 4-year-old directing our lives, just as Nick does with his milk, because of key decisions we made in our childhoods. Of course, everyone must make key decisions throughout life, but many of those made during childhood tend to be disempowering decisions we made when we were in a difficult or uncomfortable situation. Sometimes, as with Nick, those decisions are not life altering, yet many other key decisions can be life altering.

For instance, consider a child who experiences physical or verbal abuse. That young child has to make sense of what is happening. That young child most likely looks up (literally) to the parent or abuser and makes a key decision, such as, "Wow, this adult who I treasure doesn't think much of me. There must be something wrong with me."

I had an opportunity to learn this lesson from a former Army Drill Instructor. I played the drums in my school band. My band director literally was a former Drill Instructor.

Bob was a no-nonsense type of leader. I learn best through kinesthetic and auditory modes so I stopped reading music and learned by listening and doing. When I stopped reading music I lost that skill. When I was in 7th grade Bob discovered my inability to read music. He blew up and turned me inside out verbally in front of the whole class. I had nowhere to hide. If I am not careful I can still see some of that key decision of 'I am not good enough' pop up here and there. As for Bob and I, I became the number one drummer in my junior and senior year of high school. All without reading music. Could I have achieved this without walking through the fire with Bob?

Of course, not all disempowering key decisions are made in our childhood. We still can make disempowering key decisions into our adulthood, even into our golden years. We have to learn to recognize these key decisions and make a choice to release them from our lives. When I shot my thumb with a nail, I could've made a key decision that all nail guns are bad and unsafe. But I believe it would be very difficult to get them banned from the world.

What would empowering decisions look like? I worked with an adult survivor of childhood sexual abuse. With a little coaching and support she realized that because of the event she was self-reliant. A physical abuse victim decided his core truth is untouchable. Verbal abuse victims sometimes decide I know what belongs to me and what belongs to the abuser.'

How do we go about finding disempowering key decisions and changing them? We must first be curious. We need to be in tune with any conflicts inside of us. A conflict is a stirring inside that something is not quite right. We must ask ourselves if a belief is true, where does the belief come from, and does it serve our greater good?

Do we really want to keep this decision? How old were we when we decided that this was a way to live? When we answer these questions honestly we will start on the path to change.

Go ahead. Take a few minutes to consider an internal conflict. Ask yourself these questions. Write down your answers so you can refer back to it later as you proceed down the path toward change. Allow the youth in yourself to take a break and let the adult in you to start making decisions.

"Discovering that you're the one who holds the key to unlock the prison of your unhappiness is empowering. However, to free yourself, you have to recognize that you've been your own jailer. Set yourself free today."

Peggy McColl

Today's recipe
Your Truth

Ingredients
30 seeds of freedom
Your body weight in pounds of self-respect
Oodles of divinity

Directions
Plant your seeds of freedom and think about one of the definitions of freedom being the absence of something unpleasant.
Now water these seeds with 3 pounds of self-respect every day . You may add more self-respect; however, be careful, because it can produce very quick results.
Next add the oodles of divinity. The best way to do this is to watch the beauty as this new divinity mixes with the divinity you already have. Your truth is the divine within you.
This is a great recipe to share at potlucks.

CHAPTER **7**

WHY THE DIFFERENCE?

"Pain is a spiritual wakeup call showing you that there are oceans you have not yet explored. Step beyond the world you know. Reach for heights that you never thought possible."
Debbie Ford

Why is it that physical wounds are expected to heal, while emotional wounds are, at minimum, expected to take a lot of time and many are even allowed to remain infected, to fester, and grow? If I walked around with a nail in my thumb, total strangers would ask me why I did not pull It. If they did not ask me, they would surely ask themselves.

You may say that my nail was visible and the emotional wound is invisible. You may say that the nail is not meant to be left in the body, it is foreign material. It could be argued that somebody else's pains or misunderstandings are foreign objects in our bodies. Most of the emotional wounds I have seen are actually very visible.

Emotionally wounded people live with the illusion that they have secrets. Their so-called secrets become very visible through their actions. The secrets that they think they keep quiet have all been experienced by others before them, and have either been transformed, or carried to a premature grave. Just ask Karen Carpenter, Elvis Presley, Michael Jackson, and Whitney Houston about this.

"What you don't conquer, will conquer you."
Lindsay Graham

Yes, But emotional wounds are hard to get over!

That's the choice many people make. They choose to escape, deny, and carry past garbage that is not theirs for the rest of their lives. This is a form of hate -- hate of the original event, hate of self, or hate of the original perpetrator. I believe there is a second way to look at *HARD*. How about an acronym? *HEALING AND REALLY DIVINE.*

We can find the divine in ourselves as a result of the wound and nature that divinity. I have always said that hate is the only acid that eats its own container, and I choose not to have my past eating away at me or my future.

I have heard many people say, "I tried everything and I just can't change!" This statement generally means they tried a few methods that did not work for them immediately. How many inspiring stories from history do you know where the victor tried a few things and then permanently gave up? Yep. Not a single one.

One reason people hold onto their baggage is they convince themselves that they are fragile. Human beings are not fragile. We are very resilient. God gives us nothing we can't handle.

So you got a big load put on you. God knows what He is doing. God knows you can handle it. One does not have to look very hard to see that God is always inviting us to live a complete life. Again, God knew what He was doing when He put everything you want on the other side of fear.

Maybe you can't believe what God put you through. Perhaps it does no good to tell you that God only does that to the strong. Analyze that sentence. The word "through" is past tense You already went through it. You already survived the tragic event.

There can be only one person that carries what you've been though into the present. You continue to carry this by means of your focus.

Focus is a powerful tool when used to deal with the past. I find people do one of three things with focus. One, they focus on their past all the time. They relive it daily and keep experiencing the same negative emotions wrapped around the event. Now that is an acid that will eat you up! Two, they use escape and distraction to avoid thinking about the wound. The top five Go To escapes and distractions are: cigarettes, food, alcohol, drugs, and violence.

If you try to escape your true life by using distraction, your life cannot end in a happy story. Options one and two both continue to focus on the wound. You see, the brain cannot process a negative verb, so when you ask it *not* to do something, it has to do that very thing. Case in point. Do NOT think of a blue car. Were you able to avoid thinking of a blue car? See, how the negative verb was missed?

Luckily, there is a third option. You focus on what you are: a loving, powerful being and then begin to transform the wound/gift and be a better person because you walked through the fire. People who choose option three do not rent space in their heads to others.

To summarize this chapter, we generally accept wounds/gifts in a sudden, quick instant in our lives and make key decisions by assigning particular meanings to events. The most important lesson in this chapter is to stop thinking that repairing emotional wounds must take a long time.

We can release disempowering key decisions and rewrite the meaning quicker than most people think. Again, it does not have to be hard.

Your life is calling; your calling is life. Will you answer?

"Don't let your history interfere with your destiny."
                                                    Steve Maraboli

CHAPTER **8**

RIPPLES

*"Successful people ask better questions, and
as a result, they get better answers."*
Anthony Robbins

Next time you're near a body of water I want you to throw a stone into it. Do it in a manner that it does not create ripples when the stone hits the water. What? Do you think is it impossible not to send out ripples that travel out from the initial impact? I agree with you. It is impossible to act without creating consequences.

This next paragraph is very important, so I decided to type it very slowly so you would have to read it very slowly!

Why do we think we can throw actions, emotions, and thoughts around without ripples, without consequences? It, too, is impossible. For every action there is an opposite and equal reaction. It is time to stop denying physics. Harboring negative emotions in your heart and soul is no less harmful than smoking or running with scissors. All three vices will catch up to you. Please, stop and think about this.

Consequences are tied to EVERYTHING we do, positive or negative. We can do NOTHING that does not have consequences.

I allowed anger to drive my life just before three of the worst common colds I have ever had.

These three episodes, along with several other experiences, helped me recognize how I was choosing and delivering my own negative consequences, or ripples, if you will. I don't know about you, but I have had enough of experiencing the power of negative ripples. The good news is that the pendulum swings both ways! One example for me has been keeping my thought process on the optimistic side of the ledger. I avoid dwelling in negative thoughts. My peace of mind has increased many fold. I challenge you to live one day without complaining and watch what happens. I also warn you it's not easy. These days, I look forward to experiencing many more examples of positive ripples as I grow in my ability to think more positive thoughts every day.

Ripples can and do transcend generations with both healthy and unhealthy effects. We have to be very cautious with this fact and not use it as an excuse or source of blame. My personal story of ripples affecting many generations starts with my great-grandfather. Who died before I was born. He lost his wife as the last of their five children entered this world. He suddenly found himself the lone parent of five children all under the age of eight. Unfortunately, he did not have the Emotional Freedom/Fitness to deal with this sudden change. His choice sent ripples down four generations to my life.

Instead of finding a way to deal with being a single parent of five, he chose to escape; he abandoned his family. The five children were split up and farmed out to anyone who would take them. My grandfather was raised by many families, and grew up in a tough environment. He spent his youth traveling from farm to farm working for room and board.

The five children did not get back together until they were young adults. I remember my grandfather telling me that the first funeral he went to was for his best friend who was shot for stealing a watermelon. I appreciate the fact that both of these men grew up in much different times than you and I. Life was much more of a struggle for what we today take for granted. The times, however, do not excuse forgoing the reach for one's personal best. You and I also have conditions that make our time a unique struggle.

My grandfather grew up, married, and had two daughters, yet he did not pull the nail that was his childhood. He carried his tough childhood with him throughout his life. His escape became working all the time and being tough and hardened. He wanted a son, but since he had two daughters, he chose my mom to try to fill that role. He taught my mom to shadow or suppress many of her feminine qualities, and to be disappointed that she was not a boy.

My mother also chose not to pull her nail as an adult; therefore, sending the ripples to yet another generation. She married and had four children, two girls and two boys. She believed she was the identity her father gave her. Her outlook on life was, "I will be a very hard worker and be tough." She gave confusing messages to all of her children. To her daughters, she conveyed that they were not as good as boys. To her sons she tried to combat their male energy because she could never make her father happy by being a girl. She combated our male energy at times with her anger and rage. On more than one occasion the punishment did not fit the crime of typical boy behavior for my brother and me.

My mother's anger sometimes came out with profound physical consequences.

66

I remember being on the receiving end of this storm, the storm that by now had been brewing for three generations. In one painful incident I made a key decision that cost me much peace. The key decision I made was that it was not safe to urinate around others; I needed seclusion for this task. For years into my adult life I could not use public restrooms. I particularly could not use urinals. I had to use stalls. There were many times I felt the need to relieve myself, only to walk into the public restroom and walk back out with a still full bladder.

How did I come to make this painful key decision, this owning of things that were not mine but were handed down through multiple generations? The most important answer is that I chose the meaning for the situation. The next most important item is that I chose to keep that key decision far too long.

See, when I was seven-years-old, our upstairs bathroom had some plumbing problems. There was a leaky wax seal at the base of the toilet.

My brother and I were blamed repeatedly for the mess on the floor; it must have been our poor aim. My mother would drag us into the bathroom and I believe now as an adult, berate us for being what she could not be -- a boy. She would drag us into the bathroom, and start with verbal abuse and finish with physical abuse, and pure rage about our lack of aiming ability. This went on for several weeks until my father discovered the faulty wax seal and replaced it. That was when I made a disempowering key decision as a youth. I am happy to report that with self-growth and study I started to break the thought process that kept me locked in the past. I used many pattern interrupts and erased that key decision and, oh, what a relief it is.

When I reflect back on the anxiety I carried upon entering a public restroom, by staying stuck in my past, I am evermore reminded of the power of releasing baggage. The silver lining to that story is that I learned the skills needed to break my pattern, which has facilitated in helping me break other people's patterns of limiting beliefs. This is also a fine example of how easily one can allow a single traumatic life event to ripple and affect one's public life.

So what does it mean to live a life knowing that everything we do causes ripples? Personally I strive for all the pebbles I throw to have positive intents or positive ripples. *Yes, But* that is very difficult. Where did we get the impression that we get to turn away from everything that has difficulty or pain associated with it? Yes, it is difficult. We must get past fear, pain, and difficulty in order to get the prize. Although, I strive for all my pebbles to have positive ripples, I'm not there yet. I'm, by no mean's perfect. However, I do find that gaining Emotional Freedom/Fitness takes me closer, and making positive ripples gets easier as I progress further along this path.

Here are a few tips on getting a good start at monitoring the inputs in your life.
I would invite you to:
    1.) Stop judging others,
    2.) Stop judging yourself,
    3.) Stop doubting yourself,
    4.) Open up your mind, and
    5.) Stop adding junk fuel to your body.

I'm asking you to stop treating your life as if it were just a dress rehearsal. How did we get the idea that "I'll do it later" is a healthy way to approach life? Today is later!

This is your stage, your play, and you have a starring role. Step up, bring your performance to life!

Believe me this takes diligence to continuously ripple your life in powerful ways. I will give you an example of how easily I slip. I sometimes find that when I learn something new I instantly say to myself, "Why didn't I already know this? I should've known this much sooner?" I beat myself up and judge myself for learning something new. Do you suppose there are better ways to reward myself for learning something new? Perhaps instead, I could remove all judgment and simply honor and use gratitude for the fact that I will always be learning.

I use a tool to help me stay in the positive. Maybe it will help you to achieve this goal. Find two small pebbles -- one for each pocket. With a Sharpie pen, place a negative sign on one and a positive sign on the other pebble. When life throws you a challenge you can decide which pocket to reach for and which pebble to cast.
Be very careful with your thoughts and actions. They ripple out to others in wide and profound ways.

> *"You're picky about what you wear.*
> *You're picky about what you put in your*
> *mouth.*
> *Be pickier about what you think."*
> *Abraham / Esther Hicks*

Today's recipe

Potential

Ingredients
1 gallon of new standards
2 bushels of wonder
3 heaps of blessings

Directions
Consume one bushel of wonder to expand in your heart,
and then wonder about beauty, life, and miracles. Next, add
one gallon of new standards. Use the whole gallon because
once you start, more new standards will just keep coming
without buying them from an outside source.
Three heaps of blessings are a lot of blessing, so, be sure to
count them before you add them. This is very important. Do
not miss any when you are counting.
Give the extra bushel of wonder to a friend.

It takes no more effort to throw at positive pebble than a negative stone.

LET'S GET MEDICAL

"Your body hears everything your mind says."
Naomi Judd

How many times do we reject Naomi Judd's quote? I hear whispers of Chapter 8 in that quote. How many times do we not even notice the power of our thoughts over the physiology of our body? I believe most people reject the concept that thoughts or emotions affect our physical body. We say, "That is what medicine is for." What do you say we look at some everyday examples where a thought changes the body?

THE THOUGHT OR FEELING	THE PHYSICAL
1. You get embarrassed and	your cheeks turn red.
2. You think about your favorite food	and you salivate.
3. You worry and	you get ulcers.
4. You feel excited and	your pulse increases.
5. You feel angry and	your muscles tense.
6. You feel sad and	you lose energy.

How about we test this with you? Please, envision this while you sit in your chair. You are visiting the Grand Canyon on a nice, sunny day. You leave your car and there is a slight breeze at your back. As you walk closer to the cliff ledge you notice a slight grade change slanting downward to the canyon. The last six feet has some loose gravel and the wind begins to gust.

You look over the edge into the vast opening and your hat blows off your head into the nothingness. You next try to sit on the ledge but the slope is too steep so you stumble backward two steps. Do I need to take you any further? If you felt the emotion here, you also had a physical reaction as well. What did your body do? Did you move in your seat? Did you get a nasty feeling in your stomach? Did you get tense? Every moment your body is reacting to your real-life thoughts.

The abbreviated list above includes items we all accept as truth because we have all experienced them or know someone who has. They all follow the narrative, "Stop it or you will make yourself sick." The challenge arrives when I ask you to apply this same concept to the big problems of cancer, anxiety, or depression, just to name a few.

A study released in 2002 from Baylor University in Texas takes the power of the mind to the next level. Can your mind heal a problem knee that seemingly requires surgery? The study took 180 people with identical knee diagnosis and divided them into three groups. Group A received traditional surgery. Group B received a reduced surgery washing loose cartilage from the knee. Group C received placebo surgery. The doctors made the traditional incision and then stopped, nothing else was done except sewing the incision closed. The three groups were not told who received which form of surgery. They were monitored for two years to follow their progress. All three groups reported improvement. Groups A and B reported no better results than group C. In some cases Group C reported better results than group B. When someone says oh it is just the placebo effect, that person does not have a grasp on the power of the mind.

Why were we trained to reach for a pill bottle when we have personal proof of the power that thoughts can affect the body? Think about the dashboard in your car. It has wires connecting a sensor on the engine to a warning light in your dashboard. Have you ever seriously thought about cutting those wires in your car? How many people have cut the wires connecting their emotions to their bodies, thereby stopping all signals? How many of us reach for the least invasive remedy first?

Your state of mind has a direct correlation to the biochemical reactions going on in your body. In *The Biology of Belief*, Dr. Bruce Lipton discusses how he proved, with laboratory tests, that the structure of our cells is affected by how we think and behave. That is the exact opposite of the assumption that we are victims of our genes and heredity. Dr. Lipton's discovery was not news to most practitioners in the alternative healing trades. Mainstream medicine has a history of denying this but is finally warming up to Dr. Lipton's results.

While I was writing this book the news of Robin Williams' passing was reported. Robin was beloved by so many for displaying his award-winning humor and acting. I am sad to hear that Robin's death was a suicide due to severe depression. It makes me wonder. I find it ironic that in one movie Robin played a psychologist and his character stated, "the human spirit is far more powerful than any drug." Yes. It makes me wonder.

How many doctor's visits could be avoided by gaining Emotional Freedom/Fitness? The following is a simple, and possibly a very painful, example. Let's look at a man in his 40's. He doesn't really exercise; maybe he's gained a few pounds. Instead of following an ambitious plan, he ends up reacting to whatever comes along.

He works hard. He's a good citizen and a good family man. Suddenly something changes. He comes home after a hard day's work and sits down for 20 to 30 minutes. When he gets up he can't walk without pain shooting through his heels. Or as time goes by he develops corns on his toes. He goes to a podiatrist who fits him for a $300 orthotic to slip into his shoes. The podiatrist also sells him corn or bunion pads to relieve the pain. He may even purchase a plastic boot to sleep in for his plantar fasciitis, (heel pain). "If this does not fix the problem," the podiatrist says, "Come back and I will operate on your foot." Hopefully, you noticed that these are all Band-Aid approaches. They do not get to the root of the problem, to the emotions and thoughts.

So, how does Emotional Fitness/Freedom and living a balanced life fix or prevent such physical maladies as corns or plantar fasciitis? When you have Emotional Fitness/Freedom you look at the big picture. You exercise, watch what you eat, take care of the body that houses your soul, and listen to what the body is telling you. You use self-responsibility and investigate the least invasive modes of healing first rather than Band-Aid approaches. You ask what the core issue is.

> *"You must be the change that you seek in the world."*
> *Mahatma Ghandi*

I experienced these exact foot problems. I was that 40-something-year-old man. I received the medical advice described, but I knew there had to be better answers, not just Band-Aids. I kept my mind open. I kept searching until I found simple exercises to solve my painful problems. Before that, though, I released the emotional driver I was holding on to -- the need to seek other people's attention by having a problem.   76

I most likely learned that behavior when I broke my leg as an 8-year-old.

One message I learned as an eight year old was that if I was hurt I got more attention than my twin brother, and attention meant love to me. I believe medical doctors can surely tell how many people they treat daily who are really just seeking attention. This reminds me of Patty Loveless lyrics, "You can feel bad if it makes you feel better."

Once I released the emotional driver, I addressed the actual physical problem. You see, the problem was that my core muscles were too weak to get the job done, (which is true of most people); therefore, other muscles had to compensate. The compensation for weak muscles eventually led to failure and pain for me. That kind of compensation frequently leads to knee, hip, and back pain as the body is thrown out of kilter.

I used Pilates to build my core muscles with simple exercises. Eventually, I got rid of my costly orthotics as well as my sticky toes from corn pads, and avoided potential surgery all by changing my thought processes. I evaluated my disempowering key decision from my youth and found it was not serving me. Remember nothing is done without thought first.

The exact same principle I used physically is true for our thoughts. If we have weak core thoughts, (our truth), we will compensate with other thoughts, (our story). This compensation will eventually lead to failure and pain. *Yes, but,* you say,

I don't know what my truth is. I can assure you that your truth is not where you are stuck right now in pain; it is where you will be going with some simple thought changes.

What are strong core thoughts? As you read the following list of strong core thoughts, please, put aside that negative self-talk voice that wants to steal from you. A few examples of strong core thoughts include:

- I am my core truth,
- I can do anything I set my mind to,
- I am powerful beyond my imagination,
- I am energy,
- I am a giver,
- I am love.

> *"I am here for a purpose and that purpose is to grow into a mountain, not shrink to a grain of sand. Henceforth, I will apply ALL my efforts to become the highest mountain of all and I will strain my potential until it cries for mercy."*
>
> *Og Mandino*

Emotional Fitness/Freedom not only works on simple maladies like heel pain, but it also works on more serious health issues. Take a look at some of these correlations, with my brief description of each.

1. Stress/ Anxiety/ Depression
Change focus, language, and physiology and the doctor may decrease or eliminate Prozac. Many studies have shown that antidepressants work no better than placebos.

2. Clogged arteries.
Get emotional freedom to stop craving sweets. An increasing number of health studies point to sugar and not red meat as the number one culprit for high cholesterol. The one who manages his emotions manages his diet. It is possible to avoid the need for cholesterol drugs with Emotional Freedom while avoiding dangerous side effects at the same time.

3. Type 2 Diabetes
With emotional freedom people can stop eating their emotions. They can manage what they eat and satisfy their needs in a healthy way, thus releasing weight, and live life fully.

4. Overall general health
Emotional freedom can help us to better health by allowing us to create our daily lives instead of stressfully suffering through whatever comes at us. Filling one's needs in positive ways will help anybody live a happier, healthy life.

Please, understand I am not on the bandwagon that says we absolutely always create every single one of our health problems. I do believe we create many of them, though. Remember Dr. Mercola's report on the study from the CDC that nearly 85% of all maladies have an underlying, unresolved emotional issue behind them?

Which person is going to be healthier? The person who walks around happy or the one who walks around filled with anger and resentment? It is something to think about. You will not be punished FOR your anger. You will be punished BY it. Your body is not a dumping ground for outdated, negative emotions. It cannot handle them without a cost.

Your body and soul will eventually be consumed by negative emotions.

"When you're worrying you're planning.
When you are appreciating, you are planning.
What are you planning?"
                                   Abraham / Esther Hicks

Today's recipe
PASSION

Ingredients
2 gallons of vibrancy
2 gallons of reasons to live
1 bottle of anti–judgment spray
Tons of gratitude

Directions
The great thing about this recipe is that you carry all these ingredients with you at all times.

Start by spraying one blast of anti-judgment spray in your mouth.

Coat your whole life's pan with the anti-judgment spray. This allows all the other ingredients to stick to your pan, so use it liberally.

Next, reach way in the back of your cupboard, and dust off the gallons of vibrancy and reasons to live. The nice thing about these two ingredients is that they have an unlimited shelf life.

Now measure out, a cup at a time, the vibrancy and reasons to live, and add them by alternating them to your pan.

Stir in very vigorously the tons of gratitude. Make sure to use all of the gratitude, otherwise this will not work.

Bake this at outrageousness and share with everyone.

Chapter **9.9**
You Decide

Yes. Yes. Another weird chapter number. Oh well, this is what I decided. If you think about what you have read so far, there is one underlying theme in this book -- decisions. Your life today is the sum of the decisions that you have made already. When was the last time you made a big decision? The answer is one moment ago. That answer will remain the same for the rest of your life. You see, at every moment you are making decisions. These decisions truly are the building blocks of your life. With each decision, people either make themselves miserable or happy. The amount of work is the same.

All decisions are big decisions. Some people avoid, at all costs, making decisions. What they do not realize is that by not deciding, they are deciding. Let me give you an example. My neighbor Joe couldn't decide if he should try to advance into management with the company he worked for. He kept putting off the decision until one day, after 40 years of being a general laborer, Joe retired. He made his decision by default. Life decided Joe was to be in general labor. He cannot blame Life for the decision. Life waits for no one, not even Joe.

Joe's story can be viewed with the Chapter 8 Ripples lens. Everything we do has consequences. Every moment of our lives we are deciding many things. What to focus on, what meaning to assign, and what action to take. The sum of those three decisions is greater than the whole of the parts. With that said, we are no longer throwing pebbles, we are launching boulders.

It is very easy to get caught up in decisions that give us negative results. Here is what that could look like. As a youth you are wounded in some way that you think is very damaging. You make the key decision, "I will never be harmed again." Your method to achieve that goal is to seek total control. "If I create and control my little world, I will be safe." When you seek total control you are actually filling the need for comfort in a very laser-like manner. People who do this shut down many other beautiful life options to maintain this false security. They also fall short of filling other needs. Focusing all their energy on comfort forces them to create a life list filled with "won't do or won't try" items. The items on their "will do" list are scarce at best.

Many decisions made in your youth were made without you knowing you made them. This level of decision-making is not unique to a select few. We all do it. When we make a disempowering decision we then choose a coping mechanism to deal with our conflict.

What is the definition of cope? If you look it up you will find, "to struggle or deal, especially on fairly even terms or with some degree of success." The big list from Chapter Three is filled with coping methods that offer only some degree of success. How many times have you heard someone say "hey I can't live without my alcohol or cigarettes." What would life look like if we all picked coping methods that gave us not just "some" but a total degree of success? I can think of no better coping method that offers total success than a positive mental outlook i.e. Emotional Freedom/Fitness. It is our responsibility as an adult to assess our coping mechanisms.

"Your past can be a springboard or a heavy anchor you decide"

Lindsay Graham

I invite you to make decisions rather than let decisions make you. You are about to begin the last chapter of this book. I suspect that if you have made it this far, you have an interest in adding positive change to your life. I applaud you for that! You are so worth it.

So if you are ready to be better than you were yesterday, please, read Chapter 10 without any *Yes, Buts* and without any self-talk that steals from you. Most importantly, start today and don't quit making the decisions of your life!

"You can have any life experience you want, but not until you decide to have it."

Sonia Choquette

START PULLING- START HEALING

*"There are only two mistakes one can make
along the path to truth; not starting and
not going all the way."*

               Buddha

Of course, you know by now, that I pulled that nail out of my thumb. Actually, my cousin Tom pulled the nail out of my thumb. Just before he pulled it, I went into fear about, "Wow, this is going to hurt." You see nails are not supposed to be pulled easily. They are designed to hold things together and stay there. Some of what I displayed before Tom pulled it was part theater and part me just being a wuss. Of course, Tom had some fun with this and threatened to pull the nail using our 3½-foot long crowbar.

When we both settled down, Tom pulled it with his bare hands and I did not feel a thing. I was looking the other way and I did not even know when he pulled it. I didn't even believe Tom when he reported he had pulled it. So I did a little more theater and told him to pull it about three more times. I put a Band-Aid (yes, using an actual Band-Aid for its intended purpose) on my thumb and went right back to work. My thumb was somewhat stiff for about two weeks, but that was nothing compared to what it could have been. Thank you, Tom, for playing the surgeon for 60 seconds.

Now, it's your turn. What will you do with your nail? What have you done with the two fears you listed at the start of the book? While reading the book did you find other fears? Did you release at least one wrap of your blanket? Have you stood up to that negative self-talk that is stealing from you?

My purpose in writing this book was to help you move to action. The *Why* you need to do something is more important than the *How*, for the *How* will come once you have a powerful enough *Why*.

That said, following is a short list of *How*'s to help you tackle your nails, your fears.

The How's

1. Make a decision; nothing gets done without first making a decision. Decide that you can no longer carry or live with your untruths. A new decision is only a moment away!
2. Get real honest with yourself. Are you happy? Why (not)?
3. Never give up. The path is filled with potholes. You may trip, but get up and move forward again and always!
4. Set new standards. Make them inspiring!
5. Focus, focus, focus. Create a target and don't take your eyes off it!
6. Break old patterns. You can't sail in life with one foot on the dock.
7. Create new patterns/rituals. Go out and get those two small pebbles (labeled positive and negative). Don't dismiss this simple and powerful tool.

86

8. Monitor your mental state. Feeling down gets you more "bad stuff." Feeling good gets you more "good stuff."
9. LOVE YOURSELF. Tell that negative self-talk to go pick on someone its own size - small!
10. Reward yourself (with something healthy). Reinforce positive behavior.
11. Take massive action! Do everything you can to build your incredible self. Start with doing one thing new that you have never done before.
12. Ask for help. These principles should be taught in high school. Get some help with your new navigation. The easiest person to fool is yourself.

Everything you need is already inside you. However, it can be very tough to get at these shadowed parts all by yourself. That doesn't mean that this requires years of therapy. It does not have to be difficult. My clients are generally surprised at how quickly we get things done. I suggest that you get a good coach and move forward with a higher life.

Well, it looks as though we are about to wrap up this book. The ball is in your court now, as it always has been. You get to decide whether to slam it back for a lifetime of the true you or allow it to pass you by. My guess is that you have had a lifetime of playing small and sitting out. How about we try something new and jump off the porch and run like hell with the big dogs? The number one regret spoken by people on their deathbed is, "I wish I had been true to myself, the reason I came here." The clock is ticking. Are you?

So, how about we finish this book with a happy ending? I have always been a seeker. I love searching and growing my divine spark. To do this I have attended many schools and workshops.

The first workshop I attended was in Columbus, Ohio. It was a series of ten three-day weekends where I could choose all or some of them and choose them at my own pace. Each weekend class had fifteen to twenty participants, and each weekend included different people. The classes were informal with the leader at the front of the room and the chairs in a horseshoe shape facing him.

During each class, I sat in my chair like a good boy should. My four-year-old inner-child ran my show, even though I was a forty-year-old not-so-grown man. My four-year-old had shadowed the relaxed part of me and would not allow me to anything out of the norm, no way. All around me people created their space by moving their chairs to the side, and sitting or lying on the floor. Not me. No, no, no. I was wound way too tight for any of that silliness. I was staying in my comfort zone. Yes, I was safe in my chair! No, I was not comfortable! I remember thinking, "Wow, maybe sitting on the floor would be nice. Even relaxing. Is it possible for me to do that?" I asked, "What would people think? What would I think?" I don't remember how long it took, how many classes, except that it was far too many.

I finally made the jump. OK, the step because I thought I could not make a jump. First, I took off my shoes. WOW! Can you imagine the audacity? After that taste of freedom it was not long until I was fully participating and lying on the floor. I will never go back to my self-made chains.

Upon reflection and without judgment I look back and laugh that I showed up at a self-improvement class thinking that I could stay in my comfort zone. How many people show up at life, which is a continuing education class, and expect to do the same?

I will leave with this: maybe you can start with a small nail. When was the last time you challenged yourself? Maybe you can catch the bug of liberation, the bug of life! Are you a better person today than you were yesterday?

This book did not enter either your life or my life by mistake! We had this experience together for a reason. For me, as a first time author, I found that reviewing the principles and the process touched me deeply in a way I did not expect. I trust and hope that you have had a similar experience of self-discovery.

Make it count for something. And please, don't die with your song inside you!

> "If you want to succeed in life, remember this
> phrase: The Past does not equal the Future.
> Because you failed yesterday, or all day today, or
> a moment ago, or for the last six months, the last
> 16 years, or the last fifty years, doesn't mean
> anything. All that matters is-- what are you going
> to do RIGHT NOW!!!????"
> Anthony Robbins

Now I will ask for your answer to the question on the front cover. Before you answer that question ask yourself what resources will you use to formulate your answer. Is your past or present answering the question? Will your answer be based in fear? Will there be any Doubt ? Will you cheat? Will a Yes But serve you? Will you bother to answer it. Can a disempowering key decision help? Where does blame fit in?

You know at your core that it serves you to reach deep inside and allow truth, courage, honor, and most importantly LOVE to answer this with you? You see the question on the cover is as old as mankind. It has always been present and will continue to be present. You can answer this question right now. You can answer this question with a new and true pattern, and give us the answer we all know that is worthy of you. When was the last time you showed the world what is very special about you?

With Love,
Lindsay

What if I fall? Oh, but my darling.. what if you fly?

Contact Lindsay Graham at www.pullthenail.com
lindsay@pullthenail.com

Military Veterans

I offer my services free of charge, using the principles of this book for all Honorably Discharged veterans.

Additional Quotations

Love is what we are born with. Fear is what we learned here.
Marianne Williamson

Men are born to succeed, not to fail.
Henry David Thoreau

Don't wish it was easier. Wish you were better.
Jim Rohn

Your task is not to seek for love, but merely to seek and find all the barriers within yourself that you have built against it.
Rumi

The mind is everything. What you think you become.
Buddha

Problems that remain persistently insoluble should always be suspected as questions asked in the wrong way.
Alan Watts

If you are irritated by every rub, how will your mirror be polished?
The wound is the place where the Light enters you. Sit, be still, and listen, because you're drunk and we're at the edge of the roof.
I know you're tired, but come, this is the way.
What you seek seeks you.
Rumi

The more you see yourself as what you'd like to become and act as if what you want is already there, the more you'll activate those dormant forces that will collaborate to transform your dream into your reality

Wayne W. Dyer

We can easily forgive a child who is afraid of the dark. The real tragedy of life is when men are afraid of the light.

Plato

The soul never thinks without a picture.

Aristotle, Life Coach of Alexander the Great

I dream my painting and paint my dream.

Vincent Van Gogh

Good leaders create vision, articulate the vision, passionately own the vision, and relentlessly drive it to completion.

Jack Welch, former chairman of General Electric

You see, if I hold beliefs that it can happen, it will happen, it IS happening… it MUST happen. But on the other hand, if I hold beliefs that it can't happen, it isn't happening, it will never happen…it NEVER will. It's pretty simple. YOU control what you believe. You control what you think. You control what you feel. And those things CREATE REALITY.

Boni Lonnsburry

On this day of your life, I believe God wants you to know that insights come to you and through you. Wisdom does not flow only one way. You may not have thought of yourself as a source of Divine Wisdom, but you are – and before this very week is out someone will be relying on you for just that. When that moment comes, I am sure you will be ready. If you were not, the moment would not come. Therefore, trust the process and yourself.

Neale Donald Walsch

Let's affirm. Today is the start of a new adventure, and I look forward to it eagerly.

Louise Hay

ABOUT THE AUTHOR

Lindsay Graham grew up the son of a farmer and an entrepreneur. He spent time as a child doing farm work and to this day has maintained a strong connection to the land as an organic farmer raising livestock. He is an independent wood artisan and craftsman who is still active in his workshop on a commercial basis. Lindsay has owned a building moving company and served on the board of directors of his industry's international association.

Some of the highlights of Lindsay's alternative training:

-Holistic Coach program certificate from the Journeys of Wisdom organization with John McMullen, Columbus, OH
-NLP certificate from the Ohio Academy of Holistic Health.
-Advanced EFT certificate from Gary Craig's original Emofree organization.
-Certified Energy Healer, graduate of 3-year course with founder Debora Kerbow B.M. L.S.W. at Wakepoint School of Energy Healing, Colorado Springs, CO
-Strategic Intervention Life Coach certification from Anthony Robbins - Cloe Madanes training organization.

It's easy to see his sense of curiosity and his ambition to serve his client's health, (body and soul), when you look at that training list. Missing in the hard facts are what his friends see – the man who dotes on his grandkids, on his dogs, cries at movies, holds annual benefit square dances for orphans, and values his friends at their magnificent best.

Lindsay is not a medical professional, nor does he intend to offer anyone medical advice. No such advice in this book should be accepted as coming from a medical professional. He has gratefully used allopathic medical care in the past and will likely do so again. His wife is a Registered Nurse, and he is proud of her and her work.

However, Lindsay believes that relying solely on prescription drugs and medical procedures is not necessarily the only way or even always the best way to lead a strong healthy life. He intends to prevent the need for sickness care in his own life whenever possible as a preventive matter.

He believes studies have demonstrated the obvious, that many prescription drugs and sanctioned procedures rely on placebo effects for at least part of their effectiveness, if not a large part of their power to improve people's lives. Lindsay believes that the source of most illness is from underlying emotional causes, and that the Centers for Disease Control and Prevention have important studies to support that conclusion.

Made in the USA
San Bernardino, CA
28 October 2014